MUSICIAN'S HOROSCOPES

BY A MUSICIAN
FOR MUSICIANS

DUANE HUFF

Musician's Horoscopes

...By a Musician

For Musicians

By Duane Huff

Copyright © 2015 Duane Huff

PUBLISHED BY HUFF HOUSE

This book is licensed for your personal enjoyment only.
Thank you for respecting the work of this author.

ISBN: 978-0-9877505-3-2

For my Mother Betty Huff, and Grandmother, Dicey, the two most important women in my life

Musician's Horoscopes   By A Musician For Musicians

TABLE OF CONTENTS

Musician's Horoscopes   By A Musician For Musicians

Musician's Horoscopes   By A Musician For Musicians

INTRODUCTION

Musician's Horoscopes ...by a Musician for Musicians

Why Musician's Horoscopes?

We could just read what's already been written out there and try to make those 9-5 generalizations fit what we do as Musicians and Performers, but many times it just doesn't make sense. This book was written to fill that information gap because we are different in every way and in everything we do.

How will a Sign interact in a group situation -- on the road, on stage or off? What do they have to offer productively, creatively, or collectively? Do they crave the spotlight or just a piece of quiet fame?

Each Sign's Chapter includes:

Their Personality

Their Astrological House and how it rules their day to day

The body part most closely associated with that sign

How they operate within the group dynamic

Musicians and Performers of that sign

I've taken my interest in Astrology, merged it with my experience as a Musician and created Musician's Horoscopes for the Musician and Performer in you, or for you, if you have a Musician or Performer in your life. Wouldn't you like to know a little bit more about what makes us do what we do?

Peace,

Duane Huff

www.duanehuff.com

Musician's Horoscopes   By A Musician For Musicians

ARIES

MARCH 21–APRIL 19

A Masculine Fire Sign with Cardinal Energy, Aries is ruled by the planet Mars and is associated with the 1st House – the House of Self. It is the first sign on the zodiac wheel and sits directly opposite Libra.

WORD – I

Those born under the Sign of Aries are often characterized as being:

Open-minded

Enthusiastic

Outspoken

Quick to act

Ambitious

Candid

Adventurous

Energetic

Courageous

Confident

**But with the good comes the not so good
and if they're having a not so good day they
can be:**

Selfish

Stubborn

Short tempered

Impulsive

Impatient

Argumentative

Competitive

Over-confident

Resistant to directional prods

And just plain old missing in action

If there is a clear center of attention or seat to the action and there's an Aries anywhere within eye or earshot the next thing you'll find is that they're right there in the mix. If it's an argument they'll take a side or state their case; if it's a jam session they'll take it over, and if it's a party they'll soon be partying harder than anyone else. They love a challenge, and they want to come first in

everything - to be better than, bigger than, louder than, and yes, loved more than anyone else. They'll champion your cause as much as their own, and do whatever it takes to get you where you want to go. You won't have to ask, they won't take no for an answer, and they will send you on your way with no thanks required. It's just the way they do what they do.

As much as they love a challenge they sometimes bite off more than they can chew. Defeat is not an option though and they'd rather pass out than give up. They will do everything it takes to get it done and this includes marathon recording sessions, all night writing round tables, or tours that just won't quit – they'll haul their equipment, and yours if they must. There's just one little problem – their very stubborn nature won't allow them to take any helpful advice you may try to offer. They don't (believe they) need your help and they don't want it. And if for even the tiniest of seconds they feel you're not up to their standard of knowledge or behavior they will not humor you just to be nice. If they don't feel nice they don't do nice and they certainly won't do nice just to please you.

Who's running the show? Again, if there's an Aries anywhere in the mix it will either be them or they'll be running everyone ragged trying to take over. At times their aggressive ways can be quite abrasive. A fact they'll deny if challenged. They want things their way and won't spend any time really listening to or agreeing

to implement someone else's creative input. It should be acknowledged that by the time they get to this out loud way of doing things they absolutely know their stuff and they do want the best show possible for themselves, the audience, and for everyone else up on stage with them. They're "out there" they're not "out of their minds".

Ever inventive, they tend to approach everything as if it's never been done before – at the very least as if they've never seen it done before. Detail oriented, they'd also like every nitty-gritty element explained: They don't want to be dictated to, they'd just like it described please, and they'll take it from there.

Because their minds are as creative as they are they can be great songwriters; because they are as self-involved as they are they also make great soloists. New material, new remixes, new shows…they're more than happy to supply whatever you want. Care must be taken to keep them on track if rehearsals revolve heavily around already established work as they can at times be all about "I've got that. Let's move on." Be gentle with any attempts to have them refocus – remember the Aries dislike of direction.

ARIES AND THE 1ST HOUSE

This is considered the House of Self…and Self-Interest, which does describe the Aries personality in general. As the First House it denotes disposition, outlook and the way the world sees you. It's like a giant lens that brings into focus the rest of a person's astrology chart. Brought to its most basic meaning it presents those born under the Sign of Aries as being focused and this couldn't be truer. Aries' as a whole are intensely self-directed and career oriented. They know what they want and how they're going to go about getting it. They often have a very distinct plan in place for themselves in both their business and personal arenas.

ARIES RULES THE HEAD AND FACE

More often than not Aries' natives are either classically handsome or beautiful … sometimes both. If not, then there is surely something different and sexy about the way they look and carry them selves. Whatever *IT* is, they've got it. They can be more prone than most to headaches and sinus issues so "good air" is a must wherever they may be. Fortunately the days of smoky clubs and venues are almost gone and the Aries' performers among us are better for it.

ARIES IN THE GROUP DYNAMIC

Even though they are "solo" minded they adore the idea of the collective and belonging to a group. When press engagements, signings, and appearances must be attended you will find that they are on board for everything. They might be a little bit more out in front than other band members but they are very good at, and more importantly, committed to selling what the "group" *does*. As a group member they understand how and where they fit in. They understand their role as a part of the whole and will perform to the benefit of all. As the headliner they never lose sight of the fact that everyone up on the stage is contributing to their success.

As they move from project to project they usually remain upbeat and optimistic and always always believe that the next album, single, tour, gig…wherever they're going…is going to be even bigger and better. On extended or long term engagements this can be a much-needed shot of confidence and enthusiasm for additional group members.

They lead far better than they follow but have a tendency to speak before they listen to others. This is a problem if it happens all the time and should be addressed. Aries will stop (maybe just for a moment) if they're able to realize and to understand that questions

are asked of them for clarification of their directives and not refusals to comply.

As cranky as they can be sometimes, there will always be a few admirers tagging along behind them eager to do their bidding. Aries will always have their very own personal fan club members. That's just the way it's going to be.

ARIES MUSICIANS AND PERFORMERS

BACH – MARCH 21

CHAKA KHAN – MARCH 23

ARETHA FRANKLIN – MARCH 25

ELTON JOHN – MARCH 25

DIANA ROSS – MARCH 26

KENNY CHESNEY – MARCH 26

STEVEN TYLER – MARCH 26

FERGIE – MARCH 27

MARIAH CAREY – MARCH 27

LADY GAGA – MARCH 28

ERIC CLAPTON – MARCH 30

NORAH JONES – MARCH 30

GIL SCOTT-HERON – APRIL 1

MARVIN GAYE – APRIL 2

LEONA LEWIS – APRIL 3

JILL SCOTT – APRIL 4

PHARRELL WILLIAMS – APRIL 5

BILLIE HOLIDAY – APRIL 7

AKON – APRIL 16

Musician's Horoscopes   By A Musician For Musicians

SELENA – APRIL 16

VICTORIA BECKHAM – APRIL 17

TAURUS

April 20-May 20

A Feminine Earth sign with Fixed Energy, Taurus is ruled by Venus and is associated with the 2nd House – The House of Money and Possessions. It is the second sign on the zodiac wheel and sits directly opposite Scorpio.

WORD -- MINE

They are without a doubt:

Patient

Reliable

Warm-hearted

Loving

Persistent

Loyal

Sensual

Artistic

Gentle

Stable

But can also be:

Jealous

Possessive

Stubborn

Obstinate

Resentful

Inflexible

Un-enterprising

Self-indulgent

Controlling

Materialistic

Making a Taurus happy is really quite simple – keep it simple. They prefer security (where's the next gig?), they like stability (salaried is always better), they are practical (first class is cool...but just get them there please), consistency and routine (the show's the show and they don't mind playing it just the way it's supposed to be played. Over and over and over again.)

With those "likes" in mind then it follows that taking risks, waiting for something to happen, uncertainty, change and faking it on any level does not ever sit well with them. If you want to find your way out of the group they're in then engaging in any of these behaviors will

have your Taurus band mate giving you the on stage *just keep it professional*, the off stage *cold shoulder* and always holding the door open for you any time you leave to go anywhere with the hopes that each time they do… it's the last time it'll need to be done by them for you. Bye-bye.

Even though they are practical they are not cheap; they do like comfort and on occasion could be called excessive in their wants and needs. They love nice things to wear and to carry and to use and will show up with some new goods or gear right out of the blue, but not because they want to *show off* that they've got the latest of anything – they really just want it because they want it. There might not be a lot of variance between their on and off stage wardrobe beyond added special pieces for show but rest assured they will always be styling something new and fashionable. They also want the Grammy, the Tony, the MTV Music or Movie award…and platinum records…lots and lots of platinum records.

TAURUS AND THE 2ND HOUSE

The Second House is one that rules and reflects attitudes about the material world and one's personal philosophy towards money, possessions, finances, earning potential, and spending capacity. Taurus will always expect that they be paid adequately and on

time. Thinking that a Taurus doesn't know what they're worth would be a big mistake; thinking they'll take less just this one time would be an even bigger mistake. Taurus is principled and aware in all things relating to the true worth of their time, talent, and name. They also know beyond any doubt the intrinsic value of what they bring to the world. They know you can't do what they do the way that they do it. They know that in fact, the originality of their art and craft is priceless. When interacting with a Taurus talent you'd be advised to know this too.

TAURUS RULES THE THROAT AND NECK

Care and attention should be given to vocal chords and possible strain especially if singing is in the realm of talents that a Taurus is putting out there. Overuse can be an issue. Beyond this concept is the overall projection of one's voice and the ability to spread the message of what you are. When actual verbal ability is constrained then freedom of expression can be held up as well and nobody wants that. If you want to be heard, as a Taurus, then one must be mindful of one's lyric instrument.

TAURUS IN THE GROUP DYNAMIC

Because Taurus natives at heart are idealistic and want to believe that everyone they come in contact with is also pure of heart and well intentioned they can in fact be taken advantage of quite easily. Warning must be given though that they will figure it all out, and they will make you do penance for any slights you've dealt them – imagined or otherwise. In the short term their ire may not always land on the source of the irritation and could roll down the hierarchy to those with less standing in the management of things; make no mistake, if you piss them off, you, or if you're very lucky, someone else, will pay the price.

As much as they understand that you think they're just out there on stage having fun (it's that easy for them – they don't even look like they're trying) they will always bring their best to the show. If this means rehearsing till it's perfect then they will do the work needed to get you there too. They're like a foundation stone that holds up the group and they are very clear as well, on the concept of creating a combined realization of a common goal. Success for one is success for all.

Taurus natives like security and because of this may stay with a so-so gig because it's there and the money's dependable. (They like to know they can pay their bills.) But even as they strive harder and dream bigger things for themselves they also have a level of

dedication within them to always bring their own best act and performance to any stage they're on. If you're up there with them it's going to be a wonderful show to be associated with because they get the idea of "the group". They do this for themselves but they also do it for you as a fellow performer and for the audience.

Band mates have been known to give in and try to do things the way that Taurus wants them done because it's so much easier than getting in the way. Resistance is futile and the resulting seeming consensus makes Taurus happy. Management however might have a little difficulty if they don't at least consider whatever Taurus offers up with regards to the governing of the group. They're not pushy as much as they're focused on what's going on around them and where they think everyone needs to direct their energy so they can all get to where they all need to be.

You'd also be well warned to stay out of their physical spotlight and don't ever touch their equipment. It's not a *you* thing; it's just a Taurus thing.

TAURUS MUSICIANS AND PERFORMERS

LUTHER VANDROSS – APRIL 20

ROY ORBISON – APRIL 23

KELLY CLARKSON – APRIL 24

ELLA FITZGERALD – APRIL 25

TIM MCGRAW – MAY 1

JAMES BROWN – MAY 3

CHRIS BROWN – MAY 5

CRAIG DAVIS – MAY 5

ADELE – MAY 5

ENRIQUE IGLESIAS – MAY 8

BILLY JOEL – MAY 9

BONO – MAY 10

STEVIE WONDER – MAY 13

JANET JACKSON – MAY 16

KANDI BURESS – MAY 17

ENYA – MAY 17

SAM SMITH – MAY 19

CHER – MAY 20

BUSTA RHYMES – MAY 20

GEMINI
MAY 21–JUNE 20

Musician's Horoscopes   By A Musician For Musicians

A Masculine Air Sign with Mutable Energy, Gemini is ruled by the Planet Mercury and is associated with the 3rd House – the House of Communication. It is the third sign on the zodiac wheel and sits directly opposite Sagittarius.

I *THINK* THEREFORE I AM

When they're good they're very very good:

Adaptable

Intellectual

Witty

Logical

Inquisitive

Social

Imaginative

Persuasive

Spontaneous

Communicative

But when they're bad they are freaking horrible:

Nervous

Tense

Superficial

Inconsistent

Cunning

Restless

Make promises they can't keep

Exaggerate

Cold

Over thinkers

Endless Debaters (and usually talk in circles with no beginning and no end)

Gemini represents *The Twins*, and as such they like variety and being busy with more than one thing at a time – they might complain a little bit about how much they've got to do but they really do love being on the go. They also like to be needed in more than one place and in more than one way as they move fluidly between, for example, performing for one group and producing or managing another. They are quite capable

of doing more than one gig in a day and pulling it off no matter how diverse the genres are that they're working in. Despite this, Gemini may still not appear to be flexible, but they are, and are very tolerant of how others choose to live their lives. They may not be the apparent center of the party preferring to appear cool and detached on the outside (yes, even when they're a boiling pot of exuberance on the inside). To them, no matter which day, or circumstance, or location they find themselves in, the world is a giant stage and they're *on* at all times They do like having fun, telling stories and being *in* on what's happening near and far. They might not start a conversation based on current events but rest assured they know what the latest buzz is.

If you're as curious as they are they'll love to have you around to discuss things with; you cannot win a debate but they'll love you for trying. No *Diva* fits please when Gemini is in the room. Even though they are emotional creatures themselves they like to keep that under wraps and any hysterical displays will not be appreciated. They might give you a go-pass the first time but they don't like it and will not tolerate it more than once.

GEMINI AND THE 3RD HOUSE

The 3rd House is the House of Communication and this is especially fitting for Gemini as they are all about making "the connect." Trips and travel are also

governed here and Gemini musicians or performers are appreciative of the road and what it can bring them to, or, to them. They are comfortable moving among diverse cultures and consider it an opportunity as well as an integral part of the work that they do. Their story telling and conversations will be filled with tales of other countries, cities, and circumstances and can be recalled and retold with the kind of imaginative detail that makes you feel like you were there…or… wish that you had been.

GEMINI RULES THE HANDS AND BREATH

If manual dexterity is required then they've got exactly what it takes and they are talented drummers, keyboardists, guitarists, and exceptional stringed instrumentalists. If you want to connect, offer a hand massage -- they'll rarely say no. They like clean air and find any smoky or poorly ventilated venues troublesome. They are conscious of the link between well-filled lungs and controlled breathing on stress levels and their ability to perform to optimal levels.

GEMINI IN THE GROUP DYNAMIC

Gemini as a rule is able to move effortlessly within and between groups. They always set the performance bar high for themselves but also expect that everyone in the

group will do the same, or at least strive to. They will not tolerate anyone within the group that is not putting out as much effort as they themselves are and this comes from a desire to give the best show each and every time…and the next time to do it better. If it's not in their control to oust another from the group then they will most likely distance themselves as they seek performance level peers.

Gemini natives are driven by a thirst for knowledge and a desire to express themself. If they ask you something, it truly does mean that they want to know what you think. They like diversity in life and the feeling of forward motion. They like to collaborate with many but at the same time retain control of what and how they do their own thing. This can on occasion cause friction when band mates confuse their Gemini need to get their own thing right with the appearance of a desire to control everyone else. Truly, they just want things kicking on stage. A Gemini will never be unprepared at rehearsal because they'd rather prep for hours in private than appear to not know the show.

The ultimate of peacekeepers they are masters at appearing interested while remaining emotionally detached – and this is a good thing on a long or drawn out tour when everyone is standing on everyone's last nerve. Don't debate anything with them because you cannot win – they will debate the debate till you don't know verse from chorus. A Gemini anchor to normalcy

is the art of words and they can be brilliant lyricists penning emotional songs and inspired anthems. An eye for detail and an ear for tone, beat, and inflection is like a secret super power – they've got it and they'll use it for your good as well as their own if you've proven to be a loyal and trusted confidante…or if you pay them. Their ability to verbalize can also be very helpful when negotiating contracts or doing promotional interviews and appearances.

If you're new to the group you might think that you'll learn lots about music and life if you room or at least hang with them on the tour. Good luck with that; there are already two in everything they do – them, and them. They might let you enter their inner circle for a bit but they are very private individuals, and it's more likely that you just *think* you're in there, that there's a whole other deeper level is pretty much a guarantee. Truth is that the one thing you can count on is that you'll see them right there on stage where they belong every time the curtain goes up.

GEMINI MUSICIANS AND PERFORMERS

JEWEL – MAY 23

BOB DYLAN – MAY 24

PATTI LABELLE – MAY 24

MILES DAVIS – MAY 26

KYLIE MINOGUE – MAY 28

MELANIE BROWN – MAY 29

MELISSA ETHERIDGE – MAY 29

JOSEPHINE BAKER – JUNE 3

DUANE HUFF – JUNE 7

IGGY AZALEA – JUNE 7

PRINCE – JUNE 7

TOM JONES -- JUNE 7

KANYE WEST – JUNE 8

JACKIE WILSON – JUNE 9

FAITH EVANS – JUNE 10

JOSH RAMSAY – JUNE 11

ICE-CUBE – JUNE 15

TUPAC SHAKUR – JUNE 16

KENDRICK LAMAR – JUNE 17

PAUL MCARTNEY – JUNE 18

BLAKE SHELTON – JUNE 18

MACKLEMORE – JUNE 19

LIONEL RITCHIE – JUNE 20

CANCER
JUNE 21-JULY 22

A Negative Water Sign with Cardinal Energy, Cancer is ruled by the Moon and is associated with the 4th House – the House of Home. It is the fourth sign on the zodiac wheel and sits directly opposite Capricorn.

WORD – I FEEL

What we like about them:

Sensitive

Caring & nurturing

Protective

Supportive

Creative

Loving

Productive

Intuitive

Sympathetic

Charitable (always up for the free benefit performance)

What we don't like:

Moody

Worriers

Insecure

Manipulative

Fussy

Sulky

Jealous

Possessive

Dependent

Intolerant

Even though Cancer-*ites* like to plan for the future they're often too busy holding on to the past to get very far beyond the right here right now. Like their Taurus brothers and sisters they like regularity, security, and financial planning. They like to know where and when they're playing and for how much…exactly how much – a percentage of the door is a red flag for them – and one they are unlikely to thank you for waving. Is this a regular gig? Is this a sometimes gig? Are you thinking of using them when someone else can't play? That's a no-go as well. They won't be happy if they find you've

played on their need for regimen by making anything seem long term when it's not. Just give them the real info, and then back it up: they'll be yours for however you want.

They're not big fans of spontaneity, sarcasm at their expense, practical jokes or being away from home. An extended life on the road is really not a desired option but they will go out on tour if the dough is right and they have a very clear idea of when they're coming back home. They like a set list, and they'd like you to stick to it. It's not too much to ask if you ask them. The point is here that they are a solid bunch and you'll get everything out of them and more if you just put in what they need you to put in for them.

CANCER AND THE 4TH HOUSE

Cancers are the true homemakers of the Zodiac so if they are successfully tempted away from their familial base and onto tour they will make sure that there is a certain level of comfort enjoyed by all...mostly them, but they're not inherently selfish. When they get what they need in the routine department they experience an almost Zen like peace of mind – all really is good within their world. Out of necessity to their own sanity, Cancer will attempt to make a home when they can't take their own with them. Given free reign they will ensure that the back stage is an oasis of comfort and tranquility

even when tranquility to some is noise and activity. If it's what you want, Cancer will make every effort to give it to you. They like rehearsal halls and studios to be spaces that promote creativity, freedom of expression, and are empty of aggravation and drama.

CANCER RULES DIGESTIVE SYSTEMS & ELBOWS

On occasion their over-active imagination gets the better of them and they can exude an unsettling nervous energy. On occasion this nervous energy turns inward giving them all kinds of upset tummy issues…and we really don't want them to go there. If they ask you to either go with them, or help them find some sort of meditative outlet, please work with them; everyone involved will be happier in the end. Cancer natives tend to be not so much obsessed with food but … let's just say very interested. Tour stops both national and international provide many options to experiment with new to them cuisine and they're willing to do so but at the same time they do have a healthy respect for their own inner workings. As a result they tend to be adventurous but cautious when eating away from their own kitchens. Follow them anywhere and pay attention to what they're ordering, your own gut will thank you the next day. Why elbows? Who knows…but theirs are a little…fragile.

CANCER IN THE GROUP DYNAMIC

Confrontation is something to be avoided and for two reasons. One – they just don't like it and if you think that their seeming non-response means you've won, you're very wrong. Two – when they do strike back it will most likely be a wicked verbal counter attack that will leave you wishing you'd never started this exchange at all. Unfortunately for you both they dish these barbs out easier than they take them and can be quite dramatic in their emotionality. This is also known in the entertainment business as diva-like behavior and Oscar Award like performances have been known to materialize from both male and female Cancers. As far as keeping others happy on tour and within the group Crabs will celebrate everyone's birthdays and accomplishments as much as, and as if they were their own. They do tend to mother people and will actively seek out those that they think need extra care and try to make things all good. This is only a problem for those group members who don't want to be mothered. Be gentle in your rejection of their offered TLC. As much as they can see and accept how you're feeling they are woefully transparent themselves when it comes to their own emotions. Even if they are the cause of the problem in the first place they will still retreat into their shell first then come out in a vain attempt to manipulate the outcome of the situation, but if that doesn't work,

the sulking will begin making for an overall very uncomfortable group setting.

They make friends easily and develop quick relationships on the road to replace those they miss at home. This is a good thing for the group (keeps them all happy) but not so good for those left behind as they leave each port on their way to the next stop. Read into that what you want. In general, no birthday will go uncelebrated, no occasion forgotten, the lost will be found and the lonely cared for. They are intuitive on quite a progressed level and if something's not right in the group then going to a Cancer member and asking them "what do you think about...." is a very good place to start solving any problem.

CANCER MUSICIANS AND PERFORMERS

LANA DEL REY – JUNE 21

CYNDI LAUPER – JUNE 22

JASON MRAZ – JUNE 23

MICHAEL GEORGE – JUNE 25

KEVIN MCCALL – JUNE 25

ARIANA GRANDE – JUNE 26

NICOLE SCHERZINGER – JUNE 29

LENA HORNE – JUNE 30

FANTASIA BARRINO – JUNE 30

STANLEY CLARKE – JUNE 30

MISSY ELLIOT – JULY 1

DEBORAH HARRY – JULY 1

CURTIS JACKSON – JULY 6

MICHAEL HENDERSON – JULY 7

RINGO STARR – JULY 7

BECK – JULY 8

DAVID KENNEDY – JULY 8

JACK WHITE – JULY 9

JESSICA SIMPSON – JULY 10

LIL KIM – JULY 11

FATBOY SLIM – JULY 13

STEWART COPELAND – JULY 16

CARLOS SANTANA – JULY 20

YUSUF ISLAM – JULY 21

PAUL BRANDT – JULY 21

SELENA GOMEZ – JULY 22

LEO

JULY 23-AUGUST 22

A Masculine Fire Sign with Fixed Energy, Leo is ruled by the Sun and associated with the 5th House – the House of Creativity & Sex. It is the fifth sign on the zodiac wheel and sits directly opposite Aquarius.

WORD (S) – LOOK (AT ME)

What we do like about them:

Generous

Creative

Flamboyant

Broad-minded

Faithful

Ambitious

Dramatic

Self-assured

Witty

Exuberant

What we don't like:

Self-centered

Bossy

Jealous

Ruthless

Egotistical

Backstabbing

Liars

Opinionated

Vain

Patronizing

Leos, because of their close association with the Sun aren't satisfied to simply bask in the spotlight – they want to own it. They believe they are *the light*, that they were born to live in it, and though you do have their sympathy on this, you were not. They want the audience to adore them and in return they will adore their audience. Mix it all together and you've got the most perfect mutual admiration society you could ever imagine. If you've won their loyalty then understand that they now expect that same level of loyalty in return. If you love them, they will love you. NOTE: you will have

to declare your undying devotion first. They enjoy the power that this allegiance brings them, not in the manner of obeying them on specific orders or requests, but in the sense or feeling of power that then grows within their roaring Leo hearts. Simply put, it is the fuel to their fire. More than attracting notice, they want to be the centre of attention, to be admired, adored, and to be fussed over (men and women) but even beyond that, they want to be desired.

If you're not paying them the attention they feel they're due you soon will (pay) as they equate lack of attention with being ignored and being ignored drives them crazy with frustration. When frustrated, instead of giving up, they try even harder to get the acknowledgment they believe they deserve. Performance-wise, this means that they will work very very hard to provide the standard of show that their devoted fans expect from them. The reputation they've built that says "superstar" is very important. Even though they are, as a rule, very sure of their own talents and abilities they do not like competition or criticism and will retreat however briefly to lick their wounds before blasting back out of the gate with the sole intention of blasting whoever slighted them, out of the water.

To Leo, the Universe revolves around them. They believe that they are as hot to look at as the Sun itself and as a result they are very conscious of their own physical appearance and will exercise and eat right to

maintain their health. Leos are also fashion forward thinkers and on point with whatever is trending at the moment. On stage it will appear that all of this – the look, the sound, the physicality of the performance – comes quite naturally because they are that gifted. And as a rule they are, but when needed – new steps, new songs, new whatever – they have no problem putting in the time it takes to get to the point where it seems and is in fact, effortless.

LEO AND THE 5TH HOUSE

Try as they may, Leo natives cannot effectively hide their emotions. They can pretend for a short period of time but consistently faking anything on this level is rarely successful for them. They are that transparent. You'll know when you've pissed them off, hurt them or disappointed them; it's going to be all the way out there. The other side of that curtain though is that when you've made them happy, you're going to know that as well. The 5th House is one of creativity and emotion, of entertainment and the arts, and of artistic expression – it is the house of the heart, love affairs, and sex. Truthfully, as much as Leo performers perform to gain the spotlight, they also get out there because it allows them to express who they are deep down. While on stage they vibrate with emotion and a raw energy that fans cannot help but want more of.

LEO RULES THE HEART AND UPPER BACK

They always act with outward emotion and feeling but sometimes, and for reasons not always clear to themselves, they also attempt to contain their inner nature by simply holding things in. Self-preservation perhaps. This tactic is never successful for extended periods and leads to nervousness, anxiety…and more emotions. The more wound up they get the tighter and more tense they become; racing hearts, high blood pressure and muscle tensions can elevate as a result. They respond very well to touch as they find a hand on their back and a quiet verbal affirmation that all is well very soothing and centering. If you have the ability to give this small thing, they'll never forget your support.

LEO WITHIN THE GROUP DYNAMIC

Even though Leos like center stage and attention and will strive to get both, they are still very much a positive addition to any group. Even though they like to lead themselves, if the situation is such, they'll also follow your direction if it affords them ample time up front and centre and a clear acknowledgment of their contribution to the group. They love the company for what it is but they also love it for the support it gives them in their quest for personal success. They have a wonderful sense of humour, enjoy a good laugh, and get a great big kick out of having fun, as a result, after parties may

be indulgent to the point of decadent excess. They've been known to pay for everyone's all night amusement and as long as you actually say thank you and they believe that you mean it, they'll keep putting in for more than their share of the tab. (This should be monitored by someone because it won't be by them.) They will be loyal to group members and to the overall advancement of the collective as a whole. They think big and act big and thrive on the uphill climb. The synergy of the interaction between this performer and their audience will always be at the very least – captivating.

LEO MUSICIANS AND PERFORMERS

ALISON KRAUSS – JULY 23

ROC ROYAL – JULY 23

JENNIFER LOPEZ – JULY 24

MICK JAGGER – JULY 26

CHER LLOYD – JULY 28

MARTINA MCBRIDE – JULY 29

DAVID SANBORN – JULY 30

WILL CHAMPION – JULY 31

LOUIS ARMSTRONG – AUGUST 4

GERI HALLIWELL -- AUGUST 6

WHITNEY HOUSTON – AUGUST 9

JACK DEJOHNETTE – AUGUST 9

IAN ANDERSON – AUGUST 10

OSCAR PETERSON – AUGUST 15

MADONNA – AUGUST 16

LIL' ROMEO – AUGUST 19

DEMI LOVATO – AUGUST 20

TORI AMOS – AUGUST 22

COUNT BASIE – AUGUST 21

VIRGO

AUGUST 23-SEPTEMBER 22

A Feminine Earth Sign with Mutable Energy, Virgo is ruled by Mercury and is associated with the 6th House – the House of Service & Health. The 6th sign on the zodiac wheel it sits directly opposite Pisces.

WORD – CARE (ABOUT YOU, ME, AND EVERYONE ELSE)

What we like about you:

Loving

Nurturing

Precise

Tidy

Hard worker

Observant

Detailed

Helpful

Modest

What we could really do without:

Musician's Horoscopes   By A Musician For Musicians

Can be critical

Distrustful

Phobic

Reserved

Jealous

Cold

Intolerant

Self-Serving

Fussy

Guilting

Virgos like, in fact need, the security of a routine. They like the convention of rules and regulations and if there are standards and formalities in place rest assured they know each and every one of them: By heart. They don't mind following them at all and will point out as well when someone else is not toeing the line. The phrase "past practice" is one that they love and will refer to at every opportunity and usually phrased in a very "that's not the way we did it before" kind of way. By their very nature they expect that codes of conduct and expectations (personal and business) will be applied equally to all concerned. If there is a group "mission statement" or "way things should be done" they're all for

it. If neither of these is in place, by bringing a Virgo into the mix, they soon will be and this is not a bad thing because many times things around them become more organized as a simple spill over from their "way of doing things".

Even though at times they themselves seem a hot mess they prefer an air of cleanliness and neatness to be in place around them. Rest assured that despite the appearance of confusion they know exactly where everything is: sheet music, travel documents, contracts, receipts, and tax forms. Oh, you can believe they've got it; nothing is actually "missing".

If any direction you give them, or they give you, involves a time frame you should understand that it *will* be adhered to. They'll be there when you ask them to and it's in your best interest to reciprocate and show up at the time they asked you to. Despite how much they really do care about you, they still shy away from big flashy *out there* shows of affection. Sometimes, band members and fans can misinterpret this as them not caring at all. Not so. They are ever thankful and appreciative; they're just not jumping up and down about it. They don't like weakness in themselves or in others, they rarely complain about what's not going right in their own life, and they really don't want to hear anything like that from anyone else.

Virgo, as one of the caretaker signs, is very much affected by a sense of needing to work for the greater good and this can translate to an involvement with charity groups and causes.

VIRGO AND THE 6TH HOUSE

The 6th House relates to how one works with and for others. In the entertainment industry this translates to the flow of energy with and between the audience and group, stage, band, or troupe members. This outward flow of energy feeds the fires of devotion towards the Virgo artist. Observers can see and feel how much heart and soul is being put into each performance.

VIRGO RULES THE NERVOUS SYSTEM & INTESTINES

No sign knows more than Virgo the mantra of *we are what we eat*. They are very careful what they take in food wise viewing it as both sacred energy *and* the proverbial gas to a finely tuned exotic engine. In the same manner they take in food, they also absorb the wisdom of others considering that as well to be fuel for the soul. Even though they sometimes choose to ignore their own alarm system they are very much their "gut" as their intuition is sharp and discriminating. If they tell you that something doesn't feel right you'd be well

advised to pay attention. Mercury's jumpy energy sometimes rules their thoughts and they can become consumed by edgy nervousness if they focus inward instead of out.

VIRGO IN THE GROUP DYNAMIC

Virgos are communicators, doers, and caregivers and as such are a good addition to any group dynamic. They have no problem at all telling everyone else what they think is being done wrong, what needs a tweak here or a tweak there or if (and sometimes diplomacy fails them here) whether a member is not producing up to the level that they think they should be. On the other hand they are also very willing to admit to their own faults within the performance and to do the work needed to get things done right. They will hang in there to the end no matter how long it takes to make it right, whether it's writing, producing, studio work, rehearsals, routines, etc. On occasion they do have trouble making decisions but only because they are very aware that situations must be considered from all angles. If you're looking for a quick determination of set order, or track releases, of album names, or anything like that you'd better look elsewhere. Sometimes they are a little too detail-oriented.

Even as they happily take care of others they need their own space to recharge themselves – if they look like

they want to be left alone then leave them be on the tour bus and let them come back to you in their own time.

When they love someone, something, or something that they "do" they throw everything they've got into it: passion, feelings, and fire. They are capable of performing to a level that infuses the audience with unparalleled excitement. What group wouldn't want that?

VIRGO MUSICIANS AND PERFORMERS

BILAL – AUGUST 23

ELVIS COSTELLO – AUGUST 25

BRANFORD MARSALIS – AUGUST 26

ADRIAN YOUNG – AUGUST 26

TONY KANAL – AUGUST 27

SHANIA TWAIN – AUGUST 28

MICHAEL JACKSON – AUGUST 29

VAN MORRISON – AUGUST 31

GLORIA ESTEFAN – SEPTEMBER 1

BEYONCE – SEPTEMBER 4

BUDDY HOLLY – SEPTEMBER 7

CHRISSIE HYNDE – SEPTEMBER 7

AVICII – SEPTEMBER 8

PINK – SEPTEMBER 8

WIZ KHALIFA – SEPTEMBER 8

OTIS REDDING – SEPTEMBER 9

PAMELA DES BARRES – SEPTEMBER 9

HARRY CONNICK JR – SEPTEMBER 11

VICTOR WOOTEN – SEPTEMBER 11

LUDACRIS – SEPTEMBER 11

MOBY – SEPTEMBER 11

NEIL PEART – SEPTEMBER 12

JENNIFER HUDSON –SEPTEMBER 12

BARRY WHITE – SEPTEMBER 12

AMY WINEHOUSE – SEPTEMBER 14

PATSY CLINE – SEPTEMBER 15

BB KING – SEPTEMBER 16

NICK JONAS – SEPTEMBER 16

FLO RIDER – SEPTEMBER 16

MARC ANTHONY – SEPTEMBER 16

CHUCK COMEAU – SEPTEMBER 17

TRISHA YEARWOOD – SEPTEMBER 19

PHILLIP PHILLIPS – SEPTEMBER 20

FAITH HILL – SEPTEMBER 21

JASON DERULO – SEPTEMBER 21

LIBRA

SEPTEMBER 23-OCTOBER 22

Musician's Horoscopes   By A Musician For Musicians

A Masculine Air Sign with Cardinal Energy, Libra is ruled by Venus and the 7th House – the House of Partnerships, it is the 7th sign on the zodiac wheel and sits directly opposite Aries.

WORD – EQUALITY

All things in balance:

Objective

Intellectual

Independent

Principled

Respectful

Charming

Artistic

Romantic

Tasteful

Perceptive

On those days that things hang in the balance:

Opinionated

Promiscuous

Rude

Sarcastic

Play one side against the other

Aloof

Give in just to keep the peace

Undecided

Hypocritical

Tyrannical

Libra is most often depicted by a set of scales and their birth time itself falls on an equinox when light and dark are equal and this is where they like to live their lives – in the middle. They like beautiful things, the idea of love, and a really good love song. In general, they want everyone to get along and communicate with each other. Oddly, they don't necessarily need you talking *to them* to enjoy that space. They love "people" and equate friends with family and so tend to have a large circle of acquaintances and contacts. The do run in to

trouble some times when they let the lines between business, family, and friends blur to the point that one oversteps the other and feelings get hurt. Libran charm can smooth it all out though and they've no problem turning that on… or off, whatever the circumstance requires. They like expensive things and want the best equipment, the best clothes, the best accommodations etc. They are willing to pay for quality and will always "get" the best that they personally can afford.

Even though they portray themselves, or want to be looked at as even-keeled, they are more inclined to move back and forth in a debate or argument in order to prove that they can see things from all angles. They will waffle side to side until they realize that it's time to decide…then when they eventually do, there's no going back. So, and to their credit and despite the time it takes to get there, when it's done it's done. They don't like conflict, undisciplined behavior or distasteful things. Backstage dramas and after show…shows…are not for them. They'll most likely be there but they won't actually be in the thick of any action that's taking place; you'll find them on the fringe of things and probably in deep conversation with a very select few. When its time to go they love nothing more than to be hustled by security through paparazzi flash bulbs and fans screaming their names. Simply put, they just like it.

Librans are storytellers and as such are great writers, lyricists and dramatists. They have an innate ability to

put their heart and soul into their performances, more so when they're engaged in a creation of their own making. Librans know how to put on a show.

LIBRA AND THE 7TH HOUSE

The 7th House is the house of partnerships, both personal and business. It governs contracts (both sides), legal affairs, unions, and groups you align yourself with but also how you manage relationships within professional circles such as an ongoing group affiliation. The 7th House is the opposite of the 1st House where the emphasis is on *self*. Librans more so than others are aware of the necessity to work *with* as opposed to against the energy flow. They are not so selfless as to put an outside goal before their own, but they do understand how helping another to succeed also helps them. They will not seek out these opportunities but neither will they turn their back on another. Librans are also very aware of those left behind when tours or shows are extended. Even though they may travel far for the money, they never forget home base. Also, when their star hits and a career takes off, they're unlikely to leave loved ones behind and are always keenly aware of where they came from and how hard everyone there worked to get them to where they wanted to be. AKA the top.

LIBRA RULES THE LOWER BACK, BUTTOCKS & KIDNEYS

Does this mean they have beautiful butts? It might and you'll have to check that out yourself but more so it indicates a tendency to lower back problems and kidney issues. Care should be taken when heavy lifting is required. Extended periods of standing can be problematic as well so those long sets should be monitored and too soft hotel beds and too hard tour bus seats… don't even go there. Kidney function can be impaired if proper hydration is not consistently maintained. This could be a problem on a hot stage.

LIBRA WITHIN THE GROUP DYNAMIC

Librans can be judgmental but they do keep decisions they make regarding someone else's behavior, abilities, and accomplishments to them self. Always concerned with group dynamics, interaction, and relations they will do whatever they can to maintain harmony because they do not like discord on or off stage. Even though they are very invested in the group's success, a Libran will always retain a portion of independence. The thrill of chasing fame appeals to them and they will indulge in whatever activity they believe is needed to take them to the next level of their own achievement. They have a true sense of style and stage presence – left up to them

the set itself would be a thing of beauty before practicality. As born diplomats they are very good at bargaining negotiations and are not intimidated by the process at any level. Publicity, promotion (self or otherwise) and event operations are areas they also excel in. Their ability to communicate effectively with all parties involved often leads them to the boardroom negotiating contracts, recording deals, and or artist management. They treat all others with respect from the light and sound techs, to room service, to the persistent fan, to media, to their constant on the road performance companions. No one is *less than* in the Libra world. Although they are physical fitness savvy it doesn't mean they like doing physical work (like lifting their own equipment).... Wasn't someone hired to do that?

LIBRA MUSICIANS AND PERORMERS

BRUCE SPRINGSTEEN – SEPTEMBER 23

JOHN COLTRANE – SEPTEMBER 23

JERMAINE DUPRI – SEPTEMBER 23

T.I. – SEPTEMBER 25

WILL SMITH – SEPTEMBER 25

CHRISTINA MILIAN – SEPTEMBER 26

LIL WAYNE – SEPTEMBER 27

AVRIL LAVIGNE – SEPTEMBER 27

BEN E. KING – SEPTEMBER 28

PATRICE RUSHEN – SEPTEMBER 30

STING – OCTOBER 2

GWEN STEFANI – OCTOBER 3

STEVIE RAY VAUGHAN – OCTOBER 3

ASHLEE SIMPSON – OCTOBER 3

TOMMY LEE – OCTOBER 3

TALIB KWELI – OCTOBER 3

YO-YO MA – OCTOBER 7

TONI BRAXTON – OCTOBER 7

BRUNO MARS – OCTOBER 8

JOHN LENNON – OCTOBER 9

SCOTTY MCCREERY – OCTOBER 9

THELONIUS MONK – OCTOBER 10

MYA – OCTOBER 10

PAUL SIMON – OCTOBER 13

ASHANTI – OCTOBER 13

USHER – OCTOBER 14

KEYSHIA COLE – OCTOBER 15

JOHN MAYER – OCTOBER 16

EMINEM – OCTOBER 17

WYCLEF JEAN – OCTOBER 17

WYNTON MARSALIS – OCTOBER 18

NE YO – OCTOBER 18

CHUCK BERRY – OCTOBER 18

SNOOP DOGG – OCTOBER 20

TOM PETTY – OCTOBER 20

DIZZY GILLISPIE – OCTOBER 20

VIRGIL DONATI – OCTOBER 22

SHAGGY – OCTOBER 22

Musician's Horoscopes   By A Musician For Musicians

SCORPIO
OCTOBER 23-NOVEMBER 21

Musician's Horoscopes   By A Musician For Musicians

A Feminine Water Sign with Fixed Energy, Scorpio is ruled by Pluto & Mars and the 8th House, the House of Regeneration, it is the 8th sign of the zodiac wheel and sits directly opposite Taurus.

KEY WORD -- DESIRE

All things going their way:

Strong-willed

Complex

They get things done that others can't...or won't

Emotional

Generous

Thoughtful

Passionate

Loyal

Inventive

Imaginative

...and going the other way:

Stubborn

Demanding

Jealous

Possessive

Unforgiving

Secretive

Quick to suppressed anger...then simmer till a good day comes back around

Obsessive

Distracted

Suspicious

Scorpios are very often thought of or looked at as obsessed with all things sexual – if it's not involved myth has it that they're not interested. This is simply not so. What they do know, or acknowledge is that *Sex* runs everything from big business right on down to wherever you want to stop believing that it doesn't. More than the basic physical act, they understand that sensuality, or the promise of sensuality is the key to all things – from products to persons – it's who wants it, who has it, and who thinks they need it. As a whole

they continue to be a mystery to the rest of the world. Even those that work closely with a Scorpio will never truly know them completely because they are that private. A Scorpio will *tell* you what you need to know, not everything there is to *tell*. They like to know where they stand and expect that contracts, schedules, and group directions remain open and up front. If they are loyal to you (and they will be if it's deserved) they expect the very same from you.

Don't lie to them, they'll know; don't cheat on them; they'll know; don't question their sincerity or they'll cut you off. They are generous and patient though and will give you plenty of rope before they let their end **and you** go, but be warned, once that happens there's no going back. Is the legendary sting of their tail a myth as well? The question really is *do you want to take the chance of finding out?*

SCORPIO AND THE 8TH HOUSE

The 8th House is associated with regeneration and death. Death in this case being transformation and change from the old to the new. It concerns legacies and what is learned or earned, both spiritually and materially. One of the Mystical Houses it also deals with intuition; an energy that runs strong within the Scorpio heart. Sign natives often get a "feel" for situations long before the truth (good or bad) comes out and if warned

or informed by a Scorpio about what they think of something, you should take their opinion into serious consideration. They wont push you strongly in either direction and most likely aren't at all concerned by your final decision (unless it directly impacts them). They are very much an asset in your group or on your management team when determining directions, methods, and means to success.

SCORPIO RULES THE REPRODUCTIVE ORGANS

They're certainly aware of their own... and maybe yours, but it's much more involved than that. Everything comes from a seed, but to grow, a fertile planting ground must be found. A Scorpio and everything they are is that bountiful earth. They can produce anything – when they decide to do so. At times they can become overwhelmed with their own creativity and visionary excess, truly the ideas just keep on coming. The downside to this is that no matter how brilliant an idea they have, and how much ground work they've put in, if something shinier and (at the time) more attractive comes along they sometimes drop what they're doing and race off mentally and physically in that new direction. The most productive and successful Scorpions have someone at their side that can get

through to them and has mastered the art of the gentle re-focusing nudge.

SCORPIO WITHIN THE GROUP DYNAMIC

Anyone that passes on a Scorpio addition to the band because they're threatened by the power they exude would be making a fear based error. An asset to any team, when joining an established group or even starting one, their purpose is never to only uplift themselves. Deeply faithful to the cause they will do everything within their power to make whatever they're associated with succeed. The longer they stick with a project or working relationship the more likely it is to survive and grow. Their ego is never over blown and especially not self-directed -- they are simply very aware of their own strengths and weaknesses. Say what you want good or bad, they already know the score and work diligently to improve where improvement is needed. They are possessed of a memory that goes way way back so crossing them is unwise. You probably won't see an outward reaction but they're not likely to forget any wrongdoing. Complex, sexy, and mysterious, their stage presence is unparalleled: audience connection can be profound. They will not actively attempt to steal anyone's spotlight but attention will follow them and fans will be devoted. It may seem that in bringing a Scorpio on board you

would have to give up some control but this is not so at all. They are very aware of who's in charge, they understand the wealth gained within partnerships, and are invested in the group success.

As Fixed Water their ability to outwardly control their emotions is strong and this is a very useful tool in anything to do with day-to-day group business, contractual issues, and media interviews. They are night owls and intrigued by the intricacies of human nature; they love the scene and command attention on or off the stage. Most days it appears that they're not even trying, that fame and attention are easy; that life has given them exactly what they want. And most days you'd be exactly right.

SCORPIO MUSICIANS & PERFORMERS

MIGUEL – OCTOBER 23

DWIGHT YOAKIM – OCTOBER 23

ROBERT TRUJILLO – OCTOBER 23

DRAKE – OCTOBER 24

BILL WYMAN – OCTOBER 24

CIARA – OCTOBER 25

KATY PERRY – OCTOBER 25

CHAD SMITH – OCTOBER 25

MAHALIA JACKSON – OCTOBER 26

KEITH URBAN – OCATOBER 26

CLEO LAINE – OCTOBER 28

BRAD PAISLEY – OCTOBER 28

FRANK OCEAN – OCTOBER 28

MELBA MOORE – OCTOBER 29

BO BICE – NOVEMBER 1

ANTHONY KIEDIS – NOVEMBER 1

LYLE LOVETT – NOVEMBER 1

K.D. LANG – NOVEMBER 2

NELLY – NOVEMBER 2

CARTER BEAUFORD – NOVEMBER 2

ADAM ANT – NOVEMBER 3

P.DIDDY – NOVEMBER 4

JOHN PHILIP SOUSA – NOVEMBER 6

JONI MITCHELL – NOVEMBER 7

LORDE – NOVEMBER 7

TINIE TEMPAH – NOVEMBER 7

DAVID GUETTA – NOVEMBER 7

DOROTHY DANDRIDGE – NOVEMBER 9

EVE – NOVEMBER 10

MIRANDA LAMBERT – NOVEMBER 10

OMARION – NOVEMBER 12

NEIL YOUNG – NOVEMBER 12

TRAVIS BARKER – NOVEMBER 14

OBIE TRICE – NOVEMBER 14

KEVIN EUBANKS – NOVEMBER 15

CHAD KROEGER – NOVEMBER 15

PETULA CLARK – NOVEMBER 15

DIANA KRALL – NOVEMBER 16

CINDY BLACKMAN – NOVEMBER 18

FUTURE – NOVEMBER 20

COLEMAN HAWKINS – NOVEMBER 21

CARLY RAE JEPSEN – NOVEMBER 21

SAGITTARIUS

NOVEMBER 22–DECEMBER 21

Musician's Horoscopes   By A Musician For Musicians

A Masculine Fire Sign with Mutable Energy, Sagittarius is ruled by Jupiter and the 9th House, the House of Mental Exploration and Long Distance Travel, it is the 9th sign on the zodiac wheel and sits directly opposite Gemini.

WORD – OPTIMISTIC

When they are optimistic they will be:

Loyal

Impulsive

Outgoing

Enthusiastic

Honest

Passionate

Charming

Broadminded

Talkative

Adventurous

When their pessimistic light leads the way they are:

Impatient

Aggressive

Exaggerators

Unreliable

Irresponsible

Tactless

Selfish

Sarcastic

Judgmental

Unpunctual…aka…late again!

Sagittarians love freedom and the open road calls to them loudly and repeatedly. They love what they do and are at their best when they are performing something somewhere other than right here. To them, the world is their own personal theatre and taking a risk to pursue their dreams is a decision they make easily. Playing it safe and staying home is entertained only when extenuating circumstances are in play. They are committed to their friends, and to them, their band mates are their friends…there is no middle road.

This ability to throw caution to the wind and head out on tour sometimes causes problems with personal issues and situations. It is impossible to hold back a Sagittarian that wants to go somewhere and it should be noted that any outpouring of concern for their welfare could be interpreted as an attempt to control them, or jealousy, and or, that you doubt their devotion to you. The bigger problem here is that they don't like being doubted, or second-guessed, or dictated to. These are huge deal-breakers for them and in your heart of hearts you know they're going to go anyway – easier to just let go. They might not like the routine that "home" sometimes brings but they do (mostly) come back. Be aware though that not long after they return, they will be planning a road trip to the next best place to be, and that part of loving them might be figuring out how to love them from afar.

Ever the dreamer, their greatest search is for that magical moment when principle and morals embrace personal experience. If this occurs on stage then life for Sagittarius is indeed perfection as they have successfully achieved happiness, fame, and fortune doing exactly what they love to do.

SAGITTARIUS AND THE 9TH HOUSE

It's fitting that the 9th House is associated with Long Distance Travel as Sagittarians live to go somewhere and the very act of movement is comforting and familiar to them. Where others need time to get used to the local scene, the money, the accommodations, the language, the food, etc., Sagittarians acclimatize themselves to their surroundings just because they're there. The 9th House is also the House of the Higher Mind, Higher Education, Philosophy, Publishing, and the public expression of ideas; all things that capture a curious mind. Basically the amount of knowledge that they can absorb is unlimited because they are open to receiving it. As easily as they take it in, they then use it as a means to expressing their unique creative ability.

SAGITTARIUS RULES THE LIVER, HIPS & THIGHS

Road travel is not conducive to healthy living just by its very transient nature and maintaining a routine of exercise and well being can be tricky due to the often lack of time and facilities. Sagittarians are advised to consciously seek additional physical activity and to work on all those places that don't get a work out while on stage during a performance. Those, that as a rule sit while on stage, such as keyboardists and drummers

need to pay special attention to the little signals of strain the body sends in the back (extension of hips) and thighs. As the toxic waste cleaner, a sensitive liver, or one that over time becomes taxed with excess needs to be cared for...you can figure that one out.

SAGITTARIUS IN THE GROUP DYNAMIC

Sagittarians consider themselves world travelers and very often this is true. Beyond the actual travel time and distance that they do cover while on the job, they are also very much explorers of the planet and of the mind and they like to experiment with world sound and are intrigued rather than intimidated when they come across something out of their ordinary comfort zone. They like the experience of newness, of new places, and faces and spaces. On the road, they are the most likely to disappear into the native-ness of the area. If you're looking for them after the show you will more probably find them in a late night local eatery than any flashy after-party. Even if they find themselves somewhere they shouldn't be, their Mutable Energy has an easy give and easy take to it and with lucky Jupiter as their ruling planet they can survive most anything that comes their way.

Sagittarians are generally positive thinkers and well-meaning but sometimes they can at times be flippantly truthful. That you wouldn't want to know something

about yourself or your performance if you could, surprises them, and Sag thinks you should. They like to tell tales about themselves, about their past, about your combined histories, about what has been, what is, and what can be. They're generally truth tellers up to that point where they aren't getting the attention they think they should, after that exaggerations may come into play. They love to talk and to debate and to argue so their attendance on a tour bus can make it an unpredictable place to be as the direction they're coming from can change from day to day and in fact from hour to hour. They do believe in themselves and their own abilities and believe that they are a productive addition to the group and this simple confident positivity often spreads, uplifting those that need uplifting and maintaining the good spirits of the rest. How could anyone think anything less with them around?

SAGITTARIUS MUSICIANS & PERFORMERS

TINA WEYMOUTH – NOVEMBER 22

MILEY CYRUS – NOVEMBER 23

AMY GRANT – NOVEMBER 25

TINA TURNER – NOVEMBER 26

RITA ORA – NOVEMBER 26

JIMI HENDRIX – NOVEMBER 27

CHAMILLIONAIRE – NOVEMBER 28

TREY SONGZ – NOVEMBER 28

CLAY AIKEN – NOVEMBER 30

BETTE MIDLER – DECEMBER 1

JANELLE MONAE – DECEMBER 1

BRAD DELSON – DECEMBER 1

NELLY FURTADO – DECEMBER 2

CHARLIE PUTH – DECEMBER 2

BRITNEY SPEARS – DECEMBER 2

CHRISTINA AGUILERA – 18 DECEMBER

SAMMY DAVIS JR – DECEMBER 8

NICKI MINAJ – DECEMBER 8

NELLY FURTADO – DECEMBER 2

OZZY OSBOURNE – DECEMBER 3

JAY-Z – DECEMBER 4

LITTLE RICHARD – DECEMBER 5

KERI HILSON – DECEMBER 5

DAVE BRUBECK – DECEMBER 6

JIM MORRISON – DECEMBER 8

SINEAD O'CONNOR – DECEMBER 8

TRE COOL – DECEMBER 9

RAVEN-SYMONE – DECEMBER 10

MOS DEF – DECEMBER 11

DIONE WARWICK – DECEMBER 12

TAYLOR SWIFT – DECEMBER 13

TOM DELONGE – DECEMBER 13

ALANA MYCHAL HAIM – DECEMBER 15

KEITH RICHARDS – DECEMBER 18

COWBOY TROY – DECEMBER 18

BRITNEY SPEARS – DECEMBER 2

JOJO – DECEMBER 20

FRANK ZAPPA – DECEMBER 21

Capricorn

December 22–January 19

A Feminine Earth Sign with Cardinal Energy, Capricorn is ruled by Saturn and the 10th House – The House of Career and Public Standing, it is the 10th sign on the zodiac wheel and sits directly opposite Cancer.

WORD – PURPOSE

Setting forth on a sun filled day they are:

Loyal

Ambitious

Dedicated

Focused

Honest

Logical

Patient

Kind

Supportive

Smart

But when dark clouds fill the sky they are:

Anxious

Stubborn

Retaliatory

Suspicious

Controlling

Pessimistic

Calculating

Selfish

Snobby

Possessive

As a collective group Capricorns are totally about ambition: They want it all and they will work hard to get whatever it is they decide they want. To a Capricorn, succeeding and success in general is about attaining a level of accomplishment that brings with it security and financial stability. In order to do so they will bring into their camp, or group, or management team, and even their personal relationships, those persons that they believe are as ambitious as they themselves are: that are dependable, trustworthy *and* in it for the long haul. They do not want to deal with anyone who exhibits any

type of over the top behaviour or general flightiness. They will view this unpredictability as a threat to the completion of their personal master plan. They take this sort of thing very seriously. If you join the Capricorn team be careful not to try to dominate that scene or boss them about – they don't like it, they won't like you, and you'll be on the outside looking in before you get a chance to say good bye.

On a different level, those that do not know them very well will be under the false impression that their Capricorn partner or team member is so forward focused that compliments, kudos, and appreciation isn't invited or needed. Not so. They might not hit you back the same way but they will respond warmly … like with an unexpected smile. Let's not go crazy. Any initial appearance of aloofness in a group setting is simply a need to be drawn out of their safe corners and when this is done to suit them, or it's done at a speed that suits them, they eventually join in with full commitment to the cause. Even as rigid and safe thinking as they appear they still do not like to be thought of as boring and you'll find that the more time they spend with you the more at ease interactions will become: Simply put, give them a minute, and it'll all be okay.

Capricorns have a very clear idea of who they are and who they want to become. When you give them the security to do so without complaint, hold respect for their vision, and give them the authority to just go out

and get it done in whatever manner they choose, then you will have a friend for life. An important aspect to keep in mind (when you think they're leaving you behind) is that they're not interested in reaching the top so they can look back at and or down on others, they want to get there just because they want to get there. They've got the stamina to do it and to take you with them if you really want to go.

CAPRICORN AND THE 10TH HOUSE

In general, and in keeping with this house's realm, Career and Public standing, Capricorns have a very clear picture of exactly where they want to be and usually have devised a personal step by step plan to get there. They are concerned with the image they project and the opinions of their fans. They may not change much of anything if it interferes to any great extent with their own chosen course but they will definitely listen: Feedback is their Friend. The 10th House also has a great deal to do with material success in life, another thing that Capricorns are very aware of.

CAPRICORN RULES THE BONES, JOINTS, AND KNEES

Beautiful bone structure and striking facial appearances are often found with Capricorn natives. People look at them because they can't look away. No surprise here then that as a Sign they are extremely comfortable with looking good and being admired, and oohed and ahed over. They don't care that you're seeing them no deeper than surface level. It works for them. On occasion they may be prone to conditions that affect wrists, fingers, ankles and knees. They are not weak in these areas but those playing any instrument that requires precise manual dexterity may be prone to repetitive stress injuries.

CAPRICORN IN THE GROUP DYNAMIC

An inherent sense of style and a flair for fashion gives them a clear edge when determining wardrobe and stage outfitting. They care about how they look and how the group as a whole presents on stage. If they suggest you should wear something different, (on or off stage) you should listen no matter how hot you think you look wearing what you picked yourself. Capricorns are very logical people and can make sense of the emotional muddles that do tend to crop up between band mates. On occasion, when you bring a group of highly creative

people together, there can be some passionate messes and Capricorn can and will clean these up, if only to keep their own space clear of negative vibes. Beyond the satisfaction they get from achieving their own goals they also find great pleasure in helping others reach their highest levels and so make very good mentors and motivators. They will work as long and hard as it takes to make sure everyone's okay and the job gets done. When you go into the studio or rehearse with a Capricorn expect to stay until it's right…they're not leaving till it's done and won't appreciate it if *you* attempt to do so either. They believe their work as performers should be valued and that as group members, everyone should value the work of the other.

CAPRICORN MUSICIANS AND PERFORMERS

MEGHAN TRAINOR – DECEMBER 22

RICKY MARTIN – DECEMBER 24

ANNIE LENNOX – DECEMBER 25

BARBARA MANDRELL – DECEMBER 25

CAB CALLOWAY DECEMBER 25

JIMMY BUFFET – DECEMBER 25

DIDO – DECEMBER 25

JOHN LEGEND – DECEMBER 28

EARL HINES – DECEMBER 28

PABLO CASALS – DECEMBER 29

BO DIDDLEY – DECEMBER 30

ELLIE GOULDING – DECEMBER 30

MARILYN MANSON – JANUARY 5

ELVIS PRESLEY – JANUARY 8

DAVID BOWIE – JANUARY 8

JIMMY PAGE – JUANUARY 9

ROD STEWART – JANUARY 10

MARY J BLIGE – JANUARY 11

ROB ZOMBIE – JANUARY 12

PITBULL – JANUARY 15

ALIYAY – JANUARY 16

KID ROCK – JANUARY 17

JANIS JOPLIN – JANUARY 19

DOLLY PARTON – JANUARY 19

Musician's Horoscopes   By A Musician For Musicians

AQUARIUS

JANUARY 20-FEBRUARY 18

A Masculine Air Sign with Fixed Energy, Aquarius is ruled by Saturn & Uranus and associated with the 11th House – The House of Friends, Hopes, and Wishes. It is the 11th sign on the zodiac wheel and sits directly opposite Leo.

WORD (S) – I KNOW (and usually – they do)

They can be:

Playful

Friendly

Spontaneous

Open-minded

Caring

Devoted

Liberal

Tolerant

Original

Visionary

…or not so much:

Undependable

Cold

Aloof

Mean

Self-centered

Unable to commit

Judgmental

Contrary

Arrogant

Unpredictable

Look in the dictionary under "conversationalist" and you'll find a photo of an Aquarian, they are simply the best that there is at talking with, and or about, anything there is to talk about. They love to chatter, babble, gab, gossip, prattle, yap, and chew the fat… and they can go on and on and on doing it. That the act of conversing encourages interaction between levels of society and within groups of people just makes the whole idea of connecting orally even better.

They do not like to be bored or to be boring themselves, so you, being outwardly predictable or conventional in

any way will make them look elsewhere for stimulation. They will be committed to you and your cause but their attention can be drawn away by fringe causes. We're talking Indie Indie (like Off Off Off Broadway) here and the problem for the Non-Aquarian is that any attempts to contain them will be rejected. Keeping them focused and controlled is rarely an easy thing to do.

At times our Water Bearer may want to mix things up a bit on stage. They've decided they're tired of the usual routine and in voicing this (or sometimes just doing it) they can cause everyone else to get up in arms. It's not that they're anarchists as such but sometimes they do want to spread their radical little wings and fly on their own merry way. They believe that they can make things better; that *they* have the vision to improve the show. They might be right sometimes, but their delivering of this input isn't always well timed or well received. Known for being open-minded and approachable they will go out of their way to immerse themselves in, and be accepting of other cultures. They live for the differences in the world. Their fixed quality allows them to follow through with their ideas and goals but at the same time this can also result in a somewhat narrow focus as they pursue a random dream that's grabbed ahold of their attention. This in fact goes against their own natural soul process of accepting everyone's big picture because when Aquarians zero in on something there just isn't room or time for the interests of others.

This can cause issues with band mates if group projects are in the design stage where everyone's imagination and creativity is needed on point. Getting their Aquarian band mate back on track... the group track... again, might not be easily done.

AQUARIUS AND THE 11TH HOUSE

This House of Hopes and Wishes has to do with dreams, goals and intellectual pleasures and Aquarius is all over this. They don't like mind games per say but they do like the idea of creation, vision, and inspiration, or, for your average Aquarian, games of the mind. They are intrigued with the process of design, of planning the steps needed to get a project off the ground, and the mechanics of the perfect tweak that takes a venture from ordinary to over the top. They are fascinated by the notion of discovery, respectful of exploration of all kinds, and will welcome you with open arms if you share the same energy.

AQUARIUS RULES THE CIRCULATORY SYSTEM, SHINS AND ANKLES

The legs and ankles are physically the farthest point that one's circulatory system must work to move the body's life giving fluids along and the question for

Aquarians in this regard is really are you helping or hindering this process for them? Care should be taken to ensure that the heart remains healthy and activity levels remain high. Healthy pursuits should be included as often as possible and a more organic diet should be followed. Fat heavy foods should also be avoided menu permitting. Meditative calming exercises should be included (yoga, Tai Chi) to offset the physical hardships of constant travel, and as difficult an outlet to find on the road as it may be, if there is a practice out there somewhere that they can attend, a dedicated Aquarian will find it.

AQUARIUS IN THE GROUP DYNAMIC

Aquarians are not fans of showing up on time and this can cause problems with band mates regarding rehearsal and studio bookings. They absolutely do think that nothing really gets started until they get there. However, they will show up for the tour on time because going out allows them to experience the rest of the world and do it on someone else's dime, two things they truly enjoy. Although they are ready to get moving anytime and anyplace, the logistics of travel sometimes clashes with the logical because as much as they are up for the experience they also want to experience it with as much of their personal space intact as can be preserved and this is not always possible to the degree

that their comfort zone requires. You might just have to let them have their special seat, or room, or dressing room mirror but also acknowledge out loud to them that their special spot is important to them... and you want them to have it. Oddly, as much as they want to move within and be accepted by diverse crowds they also like to be, and to be seen, as unique from whichever flow of humanity they find themselves in. They want to go somewhere different but still stand out as different; it's just the Aquarian way. Because they like to immerse themselves in the culture they find themselves in, losing them to local streets while on tour should be something that is expected.

Established groups have their own flow and bringing an outspoken Aquarian into the mix can be a tricky thing to do smoothly. But they do have very strong talents that can make the initial discontent worthwhile: Their ability to forward-think and solve creative blocks, their ability to lead when others need led, their uncanny eye for spotting up coming trends, and their selective hit-picking ear. They are almost always a very valuable asset and addition to any organization.

AQUARIUS MUSICIANS AND PERFORMERS

SAM COOKE – JANUARY 22

NEIL DIAMOND – JANUARY 24

WARREN ZEVON – JANUARY 24

ALICIA KEYES – JANUARY 25

ANITA BAKER – JANUARY 26

EDDIE VAN HALEN – JANUARY 26

TRICKY – JANUARY 27

WOLFGANG MOZART – JANUARY 27

SARAH MCLACHLAN – JANUARY 28

PHIL COLLINS – JANUARY 30

JUSTIN TIMBERLAKE – JANUARY 31

SHAKIRA – FEBRUARY 2

NATALIE COLE – FEBRUARY 6

BOB MARLEY – FEBRUARY 6

GARTH BROOKS – FEBRUARY 7

ROBERTA FLACK – FEBRUARY 10

SHERYL CROW – FEBRUARY 11

BRANDY NORWOOD – FEBRUARY 11

PETER GABRIEL – FEBRUARY 13

SONNY BONO – FEBRUARY 16
ED SHEERAN – FEBRUARY 17
DR. DRE – FEBRUARY 18

Musician's Horoscopes   By A Musician For Musicians

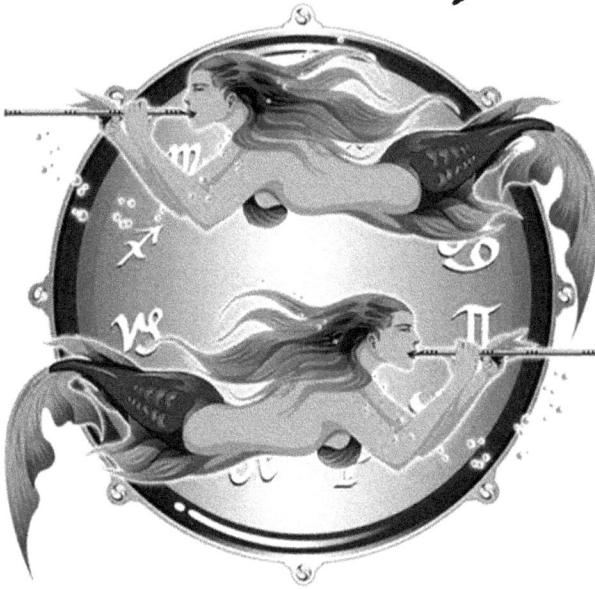

PISCES

FEBRUARY 19–MARCH 20

A Negative Water Sign with Mutable Energy, Pisces is ruled by both Jupiter and Neptune and is associated with the 12th House – The House of Secrets. It is the 12th sign on the zodiac wheel and sits directly opposite Virgo.

WORD -- BELIEVE

When they believe they can do anything they are:

Enchanting

Loving

Devoted

Reverent

Creative

Sensitive

Instinctive

Affectionate

Empathetic

Unselfish

When they're not in the mood for anything but trouble they are:

Escapists

Idealistic

Secretive

Vague

Weak-willed

Easily led

Needy

Confused

Manipulative

Unrealistic

Pisces as a whole are very intense people that thrive on being appreciated, needed, and valued, and this can be a lot to ask for from other gifted, creative, and emotional artists. Who has the time to lift this Fish up when they are busy lifting themselves up? Fortunately the built in Pisces intuition will help them find these special people because this type of interaction and acknowledgement is very important to them. In fact, it is necessary fuel to their Pisces fire. If they are ignored, left to their own

devices, or feel unloved it makes them feel vulnerable and open to attack and they deal badly with both. They need structure to keep them in line and focused, but will happily do what they're told to do if the telling is done with adoration and reverence. They'll do what you ask because they know that you love them but they still harbor a little fear that you'll abuse this. They can't help that part.

They are out there thinkers and their creative input is invaluable. They are better starters than finishers especially when they are doing something for themselves and lack of motivation creeps in. They will however, go to extreme lengths to help others ...don't abuse this knowledge either. When they hurt, they hurt deeply. They see everyone as worthy of support and can sometimes be taken advantage of by those with less than honest intentions. Pointing this out to them is most often wasted though as they do tend to know exactly what's going on when it's going on and may not appreciate your input. When the going gets tough they don't get going, they just keep going because following through on their word is very important to them, even more so than calling it quits.

Pisces natives like possessions and plenty of them, sometimes to the point of excess. They might have one guitar, or set of drums, or ... a car that they absolutely love the most but as their career progresses and financial barriers lift you'll find that they've got two or

three or ten (or more) *special* items stashed away somewhere that they like just as much. And no, they're not getting rid of any of them… ever.

PISCES AND THE 12TH HOUSE

The 12th House is known as The House of Secrets, Sorrows and Un-Doing but it is not a dark or gloomy place at all. Its greatest purpose is to reveal the limitations on life (yours) that you put in place yourself. It is the most mystical House and also the final House as it completes the circle: it is both an end and a beginning. Pisces is a very spiritual sign and one that is always seeking the true meaning of life. Pisces born persons come into this world knowing that the big question is how to enhance the experience of this life journey and that the big answer is that it should be exciting, fulfilling, and most importantly, joyful. Pisces live life this way and helping you to do the same makes them very happy.

PISCES RULES THE FEET

Pisces natives tend to have beautiful feet: sensitive to the touch and well shaped and they tend to travel through life light-footed with a definite carefree step as they make their way from place to place. Despite the obvious aspect of their aquatic symbol and being a

Water Sign, Pisces have a deeply grounded connection with Mother Earth. They stand for what they believe in. They are very aware of what they put on their feet and prefer a combo of quality, comfort and style but they'll bypass it all for the perfect pair of name brand, killer foot wear. Movement comes easy and despite intricate routines, a Pisces performer often appears to float on stage.

PISCES IN THE GROUP DYNAMIC

These Fish love to shop and shopping in another part of the world is like a bonus royalty check to them. They love it that much. If you're out on tour with them and they've vanished you'd be advised to head to the local shopping area to find them first. From Beijing's Silk Street to New York's Fifth Avenue to Toronto's eclectic Kensington Market, they know where to go to get what everyone in the group wants or needs. Bonus for the group is that they love to lead the way on this. Pisces are big day dreamers which is good when ideas are needed but not so good when they put aside whatever they were supposed to rehearse or have ready as they diverted their attention elsewhere. Compounding this is a very real tendency to procrastinate to a level that things don't get done on time and sometimes not done at all. Once they've got it, they've got it; it's getting them there, and at the same time as everyone else that can

be tricky. Their fluid personality gives them a changeability that can be disarming to band mates, as it may appear that they're not on board with the bigger band goals. They are but you're probably just going to have to take their word for it. Those not accustomed to Pisces' imaginative and creative powers may be taken aback, it does take some getting used to, but the truth is that they simply see and hear things in their minds that others do not. You'll find that anything is within the realm of their possibility and the key is to give them the freedom to just be. The trick however, is to control their attention and corral their creativity without locking them down to the point that the seeds of inspiration cannot grow. Easier said than done most days but when all the pieces fall into place the results are spectacular.

PISCES MUSICIANS AND PERFORMERS

SMOKEY ROBINSON – FEBRUARY 19

SEAL – FEBRUARY 19

DAVE WAKELING – FEBRUARY 19

RIHANNA – FEBRUARY 20

NANCY WILSON – FEBRUARY 20

KURT COBAIN – FEBRUARY 20

NINA SIMONE – FEBRUARY 21

CHARLOTTE CHURCH – FEBRUARY 21

GEORGE HARRISON – FEBRUARY 25

ERYKAH BADU – FEBRUARY 26

FATS DOMINO – FEBRUARY 26

JOHNNY CASH – FEBRUARY 26

JOSH GROBAN – FEBRUARY 27

JA RULE – FEBRUARY 29

KESHA – MARCH 1

HARRY BELAFONTE – 1 MARCH

GLENN MILLER – MARCH 1

JUSTIN BEIBER – MARCH 1

LOU REED – MARCH 2

LIL' BOW WOW – MARCH 9

CHINGY – MARCH 9

CARRIE UNDERWOOD – MARCH 10

LIZA MINELLI – MARCH 12

QUINCY JONES – MARCH 14

QUEEN LATIFAH – MARCH 18

VANESSA WILLIAMS – MARCH 18

ADAM LEVINE – MARCH 18

###

Musician's Horoscopes   By A Musician For Musicians

MUSICIAN'S HOROSCOPES

Duane Huff's Musician's Horoscopes are posted for each sign each month @ www.duanehuff.com

Here's a sample of what to expect:

Aries (March 21 - April 19)

This month you feel caught between easing off and pushing forward with any issue that comes within a beat of impacting you. So do you do nothing or do everything? Neither extreme brings you the results you want except a frustrating feeling of falling well short of the usual bar you set for yourself. The Universe slows you where you are unable to slow yourself. Accept it. Rest it. Wait for it. Bigger things come your way.

Taurus (April 20 – May 20)

You're up to your eyeballs in creative projects and tasks that others can't seem to manage without you. Go, go, go, Taurus... Until you just can't go anymore. And you probably will keep on going despite the warnings from those around you and the protests of a body and mind (yours) that you tax to the max. The process of invention and vision is to be enjoyed and is so much better without time taken up by crashing and recovering. Seriously. Take a break.

Musician's Horoscopes   By A Musician For Musicians

Gemini (May 21 – June 20)

Everywhere you look these days the world seems different than when you looked there last. This bothers you a bit. How could everything be so different? Did you not see the whole picture before (something you pride yourself on) or not accept what you did see? This also bothers you. Instead of seeing darkness where none exists consider this from the 48 Laws: *Everything Changes*. And **you** saw it, felt it and understood it first. You are, once again, ahead of the game.

Cancer (June 21 – July 22)

You're full of original ideas and innovative new sounds but you can't quite find the way to get them out of that mind of yours and in front of your audience. If, in your performing career, you're really in it to win it then take this time to fine tune the notes, the lyrics, the physicality of bringing it to the world stage. It's that simple. Hone every aspect of your craft.

Leo (July 23 – August 22)

Yes, you constantly seek the spotlight but you've still got an air of got it all together about you. These February days however find you feeling as if everyone is deliberately standing on your last nerve and you're

this close to pitching a fit that may surprise even you with the fury you spit. What? Hey, it's just your way of getting it out there that even if you're cool with most of it, there's still a line the group needs to not step over. Simple. Sometimes they just need to back the… get back on their side.

Virgo (August 23 – September 22)

You connect with your inner voices a lot, it's in your Earthy nature but right now they run from dynamic accelerato to subito and back again. They offer you no answer, no solutions, and no direction and it's making you cranky and desperate for mental answers. But, to get answers you must ask the right questions and you also don't know what to ask. Best strategy is to spend a patient and foggy month listening to the music of your mind.

Libra (September 23 – October 22)

You are most happy when you ride the middle rails of life, everyone else is happy too as they seek your opinions and advice. February though, brings you a need for quiet inner reflection but the problems of others will likely burst your bubble. Easiest plan of survival is to do what you do but reward yourself for every problem solved – new sticks, new gear, new

stage clothes, whatever you want. Just don't go broke doing it; your cash will need to keep up with their issues.

Scorpio (October 23 – November 21)

There's a buzz in your brain that's both intriguing and irritating because you can't quite pin down what it's all about. You're full of so many ideas right now but you can't find the way to bring them all to life and true to creative Scorpio form you become stuck in that place of so much to do, you don't know what to do first, so you do nothing. Seek peace first, and then observe carefully; the answers will arrive carried by coincidences that the Universe brings.

Sagittarius (November 22 – December 21)

This month you may find yourself the target of other people's problems. How could all of this be your fault? Well you are very powerful, but weather delays, missed flights, and lost equipment is really a Mercury Retrograde issue, not yours. Your best defense is to avoid the black hole their negativity creates which might make for a more solitary situation back stage but it is what it is and it is not your problem. Let it go and go have fun.

Capricorn (December 22 – January 19)

You're like an old school coffee maker percolating and bubbling on a hot plate. The thing about old school is that sometimes you have to wait for things to be ready but these good things will stay out of your reach if you try to force the process. The Universe now offers you a unique opportunity to increase your success through disciplined mastery and personal expansion. Or, you could just rehearse more if that sounds easier.

Aquarius (January 20 – February 18)

Forget winter wonderlands, you're running around making joyful noise in a creative one right now. Normally you love this state of inspired overload but frustration over finding "that one thing" begins to dampen your spirit. If you find a way to harness your imagination and realize that there's no one fixed grand answer you *will* get to where you need to be.

Pisces (February 19 – March 20)

Your vitality and potential to succeed are high this birthday month so it's the perfect time to bring to life plans, dreams, and visions that you've thought about putting into place since the beginning of the end of last year. (Figure it out.) Even though you can't see it all

right in front of you, everything is in place to make this the go ahead month for you… So, get going to getting ahead. Mercury Retrograde comes to a close February 11 easing delays. This is the time to make things in your imagination into real things in your life.

HUFFISMS
LIFE THEORIES OF THIS MUSICIAN

As the fletcher whittles and makes straight his arrows, so the master directs his straying thoughts.
Buddha

To get to greatness you must have a clear and focused vision of where you want to be. Rehearse your instrument. Release yourself.

HUFF

HUFFISMS
WWW.DUANEHUFF.COM

Flex your Musical Muscle (s)

Sometimes a gig requires you to play the same song the same way every time. It's a skill on its own, but what does it do for you and your growth as an entertainer? You need to make the effort to Flex Your Musical Muscle: listen, learn, and try new things with your instrument (including your voice). Challenging yourself off stage will help you become a better performer on stage.

Huff

To obtain the spotlight you have to put in the work. When you find the light, stand in it and claim it as yours. Above all else, believe in yourself.

Huff

Focus inward with inspriation, *not outward* with envy.

The *only one you need* to be better than *is yourself.*

HUFFISMS   www.duanehuff.com

Musician's Horoscopes   By A Musician For Musicians

I'd like to thank Huff House Publishing for supporting me through the process of bringing the Musician's Horoscopes book to life. A special thanks to my muse and astrological mentor Dicey Davis who believed in the vision as much as I did and without whose guidance this would not have been possible.

Thank you for reading my book. If you enjoyed it please consider leaving a review at your favorite retailer.

Peace

Huff

ABOUT THE AUTHOR

Native Detroiter Duane Huff's musical career spans the globe. His skill as a Drummer has taken him to The United Kingdom, Europe, Japan, Canada, China, Singapore, Russia, Australia, and to all corners of America with artists that include among others, George Clinton, Dr Dre, Snoop Dogg, The Temptations, Dramatics, Amp Fiddler, and Aretha Franklin.

As a sought after musician, he continues to travel extensively.

Duane created MUSICIAN'S HOROSCOPES for his fellow musicians and performers everywhere, and his HUFFISMS – original words of wisdom, experience and inspiration, for the performer in each and every one of us.

www.duanehuff.com

https://instagram.com/duane_huff/

https://about.me/duanehuff

EMAIL: duane@duanehuff.com

To get your Zodiac sign on a T-Shirt visit:

http://www.cafepress.com/duanehuff

www.ingramcontent.com/pod-product-compliance
Lightning Source LLC
Chambersburg PA
CBHW070810050426
42452CB00011B/1976